A FatCat Book

THE LORD'S PRAYER

For All God's Children

Art by
Natasha Kennedy

Text by
Harold L. Senkbeil

LEXHAM PRESS

ALMIGHTY AND EVERLASTING GOD

You sent your only Son to seek and to save the lost, saying through him, "Let the little children come to me, and do not hinder them, for to such belong the kingdom of God." It is not your will that even one of these little ones should perish. Bless and govern the children of your church by your Holy Spirit, that they may grow in grace and in the knowledge of your Word; protect and defend them against all danger and harm, giving your holy angels charge over them; through Jesus Christ, your Son, our Lord.

AMEN.

What is FatCat?

How can anyone, no matter how young or old, grasp the message of the Bible? The church's answer has always been the catechism.

Maybe "catechism" sounds like a scary word. But it shouldn't! The catechism teaches us what the Bible teaches us: our faith. The church's catechism is the central texts of faith—the Apostles' Creed, the Ten Commandments, and the Lord's Prayer.

The catechism is "fat." It's bursting at the seams with meaning, challenge, and comfort. It's concise, but it's also deep. Most importantly, it should be familiar.

FatCat is our way of making the catechism approachable. And so this book has an actual fat cat hidden throughout. Search for him with your child as you enjoy this book together, and hide the words of the catechism in your heart.

"The unfolding of your words gives light; it imparts understanding to the simple."
Psalm 119:130

OUR FATHER
WHO ART IN HEAVEN

Lord, teach us to pray.
Our Father in heaven.

Who is Our Father in heaven?
God is Jesus' Father.
Because Jesus is our brother, God is our Father too.

Is he far away? No!
In his word he is near to us.
Like a loving father, he invites us to come and talk with him
    in prayer about anything and everything.
He is eager to hear all our questions, fears, and joys.

Our Father in heaven, you love us just like you love Jesus.
Help us trust you with anything and everything.

HALLOWED BE THY NAME

Lord, teach us to pray.
Hallowed be your name.

Can we make God's name holy? No!
God's name is already holy.
His word and name make us holy too.

That's why Jesus was born of the Virgin Mary.
He came to give us life.
He came to share his name and word with us.

Because we are named with God's name and believe his word,
    our lives show his holiness.

Our Father in heaven, you love us just like you love Jesus.
Make us holy by your name and word!

THY KINGDOM COME

Lord, teach us to pray.
Your kingdom come.

Can we make God's kingdom come? No!
His kingdom comes all by itself.

Where is God's kingdom?
Wherever Jesus is, there he rules as King.
He brings us life and forgiveness, peace and salvation.
That's why we pray for God's kingdom to come.

When we pray for God's kingdom to come,
he sends his Holy Spirit to us,
so we believe God's holy word and live godly lives.

Our Father in heaven, you love us just like
   you love Jesus.
Give us your Spirit so we can
   believe and obey your holy word!

Lord, teach us to pray.
Your will be done on earth as in heaven.

How do we know God's will?
God's word reveals his will to us.
Is it dark and scary? No!
It's good and gracious.

God cares about what happens on earth.
That's why he sent his Son Jesus for us all.
God wants to seek and save everyone and bring them into his kingdom.
That's why we pray with Jesus, "Not my will but yours be done"—
because God wants to stop every evil that battles his holy word and kingdom.

Our Father in heaven, you love us just like you love Jesus.
Give us your Spirit so we believe and obey your holy will.

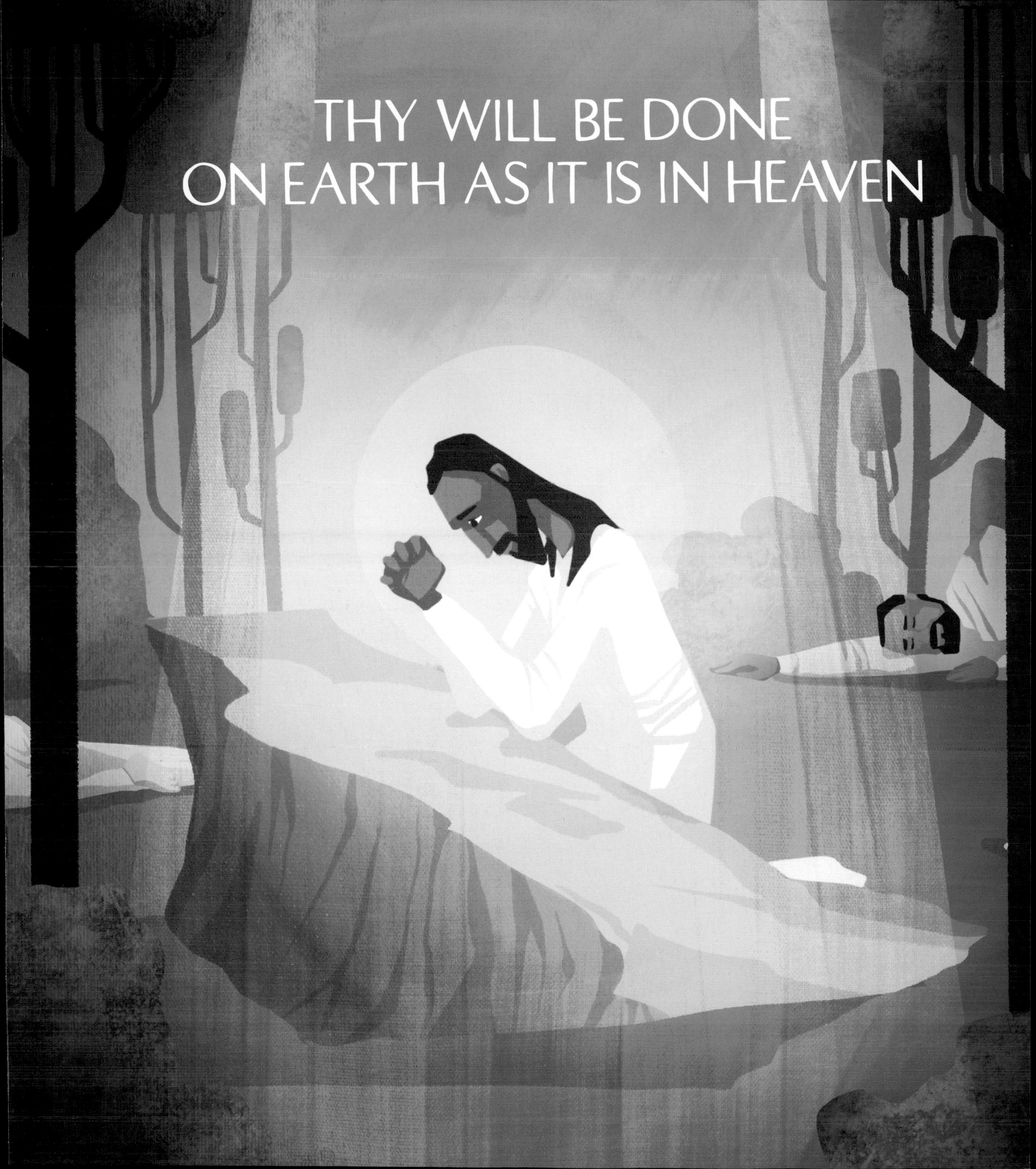
THY WILL BE DONE
ON EARTH AS IT IS IN HEAVEN

GIVE US THIS DAY OUR DAILY BREAD

Lord, teach us to pray.
Give us today our daily bread.

What is daily bread?
Is it just food in our mouths? No!
Daily bread is everything we need to live.

Jesus fed thousands with just five loaves and two fish.
God opens his hand and satisfies the needs of every creature—
    both animals and people.

God knows us and gives us everything we need to live.
That's not just food and home,
but family and friends, peace and health, and every good.

Our Father in heaven, you love us just like you love Jesus.
Help us see your gifts and be thankful.

AND FORGIVE US OUR TRESPASSES AS WE FORGIVE THOSE WHO TRESPASS AGAINST US

Lord, teach us to pray.
Forgive us our sins
   as we forgive those who sin against us.

Why should God give us anything?
Do we deserve his love? No!
We've sinned a lot.
We don't deserve anything we ask for.

We can ask these things only
   because Jesus washes away our sins and gives us life.
His blood is given and shed for us for the forgiveness of sins.
God surely hears our prayers and forgives us for Jesus' sake.
Because God forgives us, we forgive others.

Our Father in heaven, you love us just like you love Jesus.
Forgive us our sins and help us forgive others too.

AND LEAD US NOT INTO TEMPTATION

Lord, teach us to pray.
Lead us not into temptation.

Does God tempt us? No!
He is our loving Father.
We are tempted by the devil, our sinful hearts,
  and the evil world around us.

Even Jesus was tempted by Satan for forty days.
He fought against Satan with the word of God.
The word of God guards us against Satan too.
Our only comfort in trouble is God's word.

Our Father in heaven, you love us just like you love Jesus.
Send your holy angels to strengthen us and lead us by your word.

BUT DELIVER US FROM EVIL

Lord, teach us to pray.
Deliver us from evil.

Will we always be happy? No!
Sometimes bad things happen in our broken world.
The devil always wants to harm us,
but God only wants good for us.

Jesus is the Lord of the wind and waves,
　our Savior and our King.
He loves us and leads us safely
　through every evil of body and soul.
Not even death can separate us from his love.
In the end he will bring us to himself in heaven.

Our Father in heaven, you love us just like you love Jesus.
Send your holy angels to guard us all life long
　and give us victory.

FOR THINE IS THE KINGDOM AND THE POWER AND THE GLORY FOREVER AND EVER

Lord, teach us to pray.
For the kingdom, the power, and the glory are yours now and forever.

Does God ever change his mind? No!
God isn't like us; his word endures forever.
We can count on him to keep his word to us
    in Jesus Christ his Son.
He will bring us safely through every danger in this world.
In the end he will raise us up from death to live with joy
    forever in his kingdom—
together with the Father, Son, and Spirit,
    and all the saints in glory everlasting.

Our Father in heaven, you love us just like you love Jesus.
Hear our prayer and bring us safely through all our troubles
    to be with you forever.

AMEN

Lord, teach us to pray.
Amen.

Does God really hear us when we pray? Yes!
He is always more eager
   to listen than we are to pray.
We can be sure he hears our prayers,
because we have his command and promise:
"Call upon me in the day of trouble
   and I will deliver you."
That's why we can say "Amen,"
because God's promises are always true and sure.

Our Father in heaven, you love us just like
   you love Jesus. Amen! Amen!

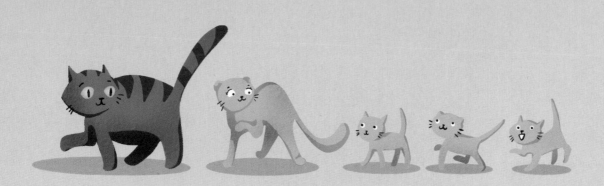

Families are little churches.

We pray together. We bring our sin and sadness, our joy and faith to the Lord our God. We read the Bible together. We hear Jesus' promises for us. And we forgive each other, because God, in Christ, has forgiven us.

The family is where catechesis (or instruction) in the basics of the Christian faith has taken place throughout the history of the church. This instruction has been built on what's called the "catechism"—that is, the Apostles' Creed, the Lord's Prayer, and the Ten Commandments. "Although I'm indeed an old doctor," Martin Luther said, "I never move on from the childish doctrine of the Ten Commandments and the Apostles' Creed and the Lord's Prayer. I still daily learn and pray them with my little Hans and my little Lena."

Catechesis can be as simple as praying the very words of the catechism. In worship, we sanctify our lives, days, and families by God's word and prayer (1 Timothy 4:5).

So here's a small service for family prayer for you and your children as you grow in the simple teaching of the Bible and the Lord's Prayer.

This brief service of family prayer is designed to be prayed responsively. The leader reads the plain text; everyone reads the bold text. Even though your children might not be readers yet, they'll learn these words as you repeat them again and again each day. You could use it in the morning or evening—or anytime you and your children read this book.

Family Prayer

In the name of the Father
and of the Son and of the Holy Spirit.
Amen.

The LORD is good,
his love endures forever.   Psalm 100:5

I hope in your word.
I am yours; save me.   Psalm 119:81, 94

The LORD is good,
his love endures forever.   Psalm 100:5

Blessed be the Lord,
who daily bears us up;
God is our salvation.   Psalm 68:19

The LORD is good,
his love endures forever.   Psalm 100:5

Lord, have mercy.

Christ, have mercy.

Lord, have Mercy.   Mark 10:47; Psalm 123:3

Lord, remember us in your kingdom,
and teach us to pray:

**Our Father who art in heaven,
hallowed be thy name,
thy kingdom come,
thy will be done
     on earth as it is in heaven;
give us this day our daily bread;
and forgive us our trespasses
     as we forgive those who trespass against us;
and lead us not into temptation,
but deliver us from evil.**   Matthew 6:9–13
**For thine is the kingdom
  and the power and the glory
  forever and ever.
Amen.**

God is our loving Father.

He wants to hear our questions, fears, and joys.

Let us boldly offer our prayers for others and ourselves to God:

Parents, you might prompt your children's
prayers by asking questions like:

What are you thankful for?
What are you afraid of?
What do you want to tell God?

You might also pray the words of the Bible,
especially the Lord's Prayer, or the Apostles' Creed.
Make these words your own!

Into your hands, O Lord, I commend myself, my body and soul, and all things. Let your holy angels be with me that the evil foe may have no power over me. Amen.

Let us bless the LORD.

Thanks be to God.

The grace of our Lord Jesus Christ and the love of God
and the communion of the Holy Spirit be with us all.

2 Corinthians 13:14

Amen.

To Parents

It's daunting to illustrate the Lord's Prayer. The art needs to invite children into this prayer of Jesus and his awesome words. At the same time the art must be faithful to the words our God has spoken to us. To avoid slipping into speculation, God's word was set as the center and boundary of this book's art. As the psalmist says, "In your light we see light" (Psalm 36:9).

Our hope is that these images might spark your biblical imagination as you pray the words of the Lord's Prayer. At points, listening to the church's saints—for example, Martin Luther in his Small Catechism—stirred up our own biblical imaginations. No doubt, you too will be encouraged and challenged by what the church's great cloud of witnesses has said about the Bible and the Lord's Prayer!

As an aid to your lifelong exploration of the Lord's Prayer, here are some of the passages that shaped and limited this book's art and words.

Our Father who art in heaven

Matthew 18:1–10	Psalm 124:8	
Matthew 19:13–15	Mark 10:13–16	Luke 18:15–17

hallowed be thy name

Luke 2:1–7	Jeremiah 14:9	Zechariah 14:9
Psalm 29:2		

thy kingdom come

John 20:19–23	Isaiah 9:6	Psalm 145:10–13

thy will be done, on earth as it is in heaven

Matthew 26:36–46	Mark 13:32–42	Luke 22:40–46
Luke 19:10	Ezekiel 18:23	Psalm 51:10–15

give us this day our daily bread

Matthew 14:13-21	Mark 6:32-44	Luke 9:10-17
John 6:1-13	Psalm 145:16	

and forgive us our trespasses
as we forgive those who trespass against us

Luke 23:32-39	Matthew 26:28	Ephesians 4:32
Psalm 86:5		

and lead us not into temptation

Matthew 4:1-11	Mark 1:12-13	Luke 4:1-13
Psalm 34:7	Psalm 91:11	Psalm 119:50

but deliver us from evil

Matthew 8:23-27	Mark 4:36-41	Luke 8:22-25
Romans 8:31-39	Psalm 34:7	Psalm 91:11

For thine is the kingdom and the power and the glory forever and ever

John 11:25-26	Isaiah 40:8	Ezekiel 37:1-14
Titus 1:2	Psalm 36:9	Psalm 46:1
Psalm 48:14	Psalm 50:15	

Amen

Psalm 50:15	2 Corinthians 1:20

The Lord's Prayer: For All God's Children
A FatCat Book

Copyright 2022 Lexham Press

Lexham Press, 1313 Commercial St., Bellingham, Washington 98225
LexhamPress.com

The prayer beginning "Almighty and everlasting God" is adapted from Collect 14, "For the Children of the Church," in *Church Book for the Use of Evangelical Lutheran Congregations* (Lutheran Book Store, 1868), 92–93; quoting Luke 19:10; Luke 18:16; Matthew 18:14.

Printed in China.
ISBN 9781683596455
Library of Congress Control Number 2022932266

Series Editor: Todd Hains
Lexham Editorial: Abigail Stocker, Kelsey Matthews, Lindsay John Kennedy, Veronica Hains
Cover Design: Natasha Kennedy

This book is typeset in FatCat.

In loving memory of
Jane Frances Nesset Senkbeil
January 1, 1947–December 20, 2021

Precious in the sight of the Lord
is the death of his saints.
Psalm 116:15